Talking With the Dead

with love

ANNE CALDWELL

Anne
feb 2011

INDEPENDENT INNOVATIVE INTERNATIONAL

Published by Cinnamon Press
Meirion House, Glan yr afon, Tanygrisiau
Blaenau Ffestiniog, Gwynedd, LL41 3SU
www.cinnamonpress.com

Designed and typeset in Palatino by Cinnamon Press. Cover
design by Cottia Fortune-Wood from original artwork 'House' by
Aleksandr Tkachuk, agency © Dreamstime.com. Printed in Poland
Cinnamon Press is represented in the UK by Inpress Ltd
www.inpressbooks.co.uk and in Wales by the Welsh Books
Council www.cllc.org.uk.

Acknowledgments

Acknowledgements are due to the editors of the following
publications in which some of the poems first appeared: *Poetry
Wales, Hanging Johnny, Magma, The North, Red Ink, Rain Dog*. Some
poems also appeared in anthologies: *The Ground Beneath Her Feet*,
(Cinnamon) *In the Telling* (Cinnamon), *Only Connect* (Cinnamon)
The Visitors (Cinnamon) and, in pamphlet form; *Slug Language*
(Happenstance 2008).

Heartfelt thanks to Alicia Stubbersfield, Sarah Corbett and Polly
Blackley and my fellow 'Poets with a Kick,' Amanda Dalton, Liz
Almond and Sally Baker.

Contents

The Underwater House

Airwaves

Talking With the Dead

to Anton and Midge

The Underwater House

The Underwater House

1. Going Under

After my house slipped into the sea
I became a landlubber's rumour

like the Lyonesse bells, ringing
below the waves to the Scilly Isles,

or Cleopatra's royal quarters
off the shores of Alexandria.

A year later, my Siamese grew webbed paws,
spent hours with his fur slicked back,

pouncing on crabs, or skittering after
anything quick and skinny and silver.

2. Glazing Over

Like a long-distance swimmer or exiled monarch,
I've lived for more decades than I care to remember,
with my port-holes and my Velux
and my tight-fitting frames.

I'm a Cromer fisherman's daughter.
Up *there*, neighbours complained
that UVPC ruined a home's character
but down here, it's a godsend.

I lunch alone on molluscs and clams,
fish roe and lava bread's strong, iodine bite.
Last Spring, a salt-marsh lamb
slipped off the cliff like a gift.

The flesh was pink and steaming in the pan
and did not smell of fish.

3. Inventory

I have three wetsuits, two pairs of black flippers,
and a face mask that leaks in winter swells.

My oxygen tanks are stacked against
Mother's umbrella stand near the porch air-lock.

Yesterday, I slung my last coat out into the current-
red lining zigzagged with salt-water slime.

4. Keeping Your Head Below Water

Alice says she can see my chimney
smoking at low tide.

She tells me The Ministry mistake it
for something foreign- a submarine perhaps
with fat missiles slung low in its hold
like a clutch of salmonella-eggs.

I have to be watchful. Collect driftwood
when the beach is a blank-paged notebook
belonging to The Drowned.

5. Undersea Cultivation

Derek Jarman, eat your heart out!
All that dried-out washed-up flotsam and jetsam.
All those drought-loving, po-faced plants!

My lawn is a forest of kelp,
sea anemone wink like ruby lips in my rockery,
the allotment's crammed with mussel beds,
sea cucumber, sargassum, and wakamé.

My lobsters hatch by moonlight
in a sunken cage:
one barnacled girl is forty-eight,
her belly jellied with offspring.

6. A Rubber Suit and a Portion of Bream

I had a lover for a while named George —
a salvage specialist who front-crawled
into my sea-bed by mistake.
He took the wrong turn by the wreck of the SS Salway,
flooded the doorway as I shoved my shoulder
hard against the rubber seal.
Foam swilled over my blue-striped runner down to the pantry.
I cooked him a fillet of bream and offered
a china cup brimming with fennel.
He was my regular Sunday guest, his snorkel
tap-tap tapping on the porch, loitering there
like Jeremy Fisher with his muscular, sinewy legs.

One month later, I could stand it no longer.
I unpeeled his rubber suit like a banana. His cock
was a fat whelk sliding into the silk of my vagina.
My whole body puddled,
then cork-screwed with pleasure.
Our skin was cool as a porpoise's flank
and his buttocks were giant pearls.
My Mark Anthony slept deeply—
star-fished over the bed, snoring slightly.
I dreamed of us herding sea-cows
in the Mid Atlantic Ridge. We could cable-knit
Ganseys together in the autumn nights.

7. Asps and Baskets

I woke as light filtered through the bladder-wrack.
His wet suit was gone.
A note by the lamp swam before my eyes:

Sunlight, dry land, vitamin D,
I don't want the watery blueness
of your love. I want a woman to warm me.

He'd taken oxygen,
and a whaler's harpoon
that belonged to my father.

I sulked like the lobster trapped in her pot
and fed the cat succulent fish heads.
I scythed the algae and sewed the nets.

I whitewashed the bathroom
with fungicide paint.
I wound a sea-snake around my wrist.

8. Siren

I dreamt a fishmonger sneaked in last night
and scored me delicately with his knife.
There are slits in my cheeks.

I run my fingers over the bed linen.
My legs are fused;
silver scales rub against cotton

and I flop on the bedroom rug,
shimmy to the porch, breathe in the brine.
My lungs are flooded like a reef.

I flick the windows open with my tail
and my diver's gear floats
away on the tide.

This old house settles deeper
into the sandbank. Copper bottomed pots
and pans are battering the Belfast sink.

I swim into the garden and free the lobster,
unwinding the rubber bands
that grip her claws.

Corkmacsherry

Ring Head

The stink of it: salt and sludge,
green slime, a rim of polystyrene,
Vittel bottles and glass ground smooth.

There's an egret poised on one leg
and a cloud of dunlins wheeling over
the mud-slung channel.

Rosscarberry

A cormorant swings out from Galley Head,
skimming the Gulf Stream -
her neck fully extended.

She has mouths to feed
and carries her fish with such grace
I catch my breath.

Drombeg Stone Circle

The last time the tide was on the rise,
the ice broke up. I think of a woman
in a woollen cape, hair plaited tight

against her scalp. She knelt before
a scorched pot heavy with her son's ashes,
witnessed her village flood.

Round the coast, the sea sliced Ireland
from England, cutting off
the possibility of wild cats and snakes.

Stretching the Canvas

My homeland is a faint smudge of charcoal,
the scrum of Liverpool dock fading from memory.

I watch that warm frill of silt as the River Mersey
empties her sandy skirts into the brine.

Wind tugs the loose canvas of the Irish Sea,
The *Aquatania* pitches in the swell like a pot of paint.

Thousands of knuckles have gripped this rail,
watched the watercolour of their country slip from sight.

My stomach churns like a steam turbine,
breath pinched by a thumb and forefinger of fear.

The edge of my ticket
imprints itself through the silk lining

where you used to
stroke my thighs, sketch my white skin.

I was the palest woman you'd ever seen;
your soft, tapered fingers like sable brushes,

the fingers of a man who'd never laboured,
knew to ask a woman what she liked.

You named me your water sprite,
traced blue streams on my skin's map,

murmured you wouldn't let me out of view
in case I grew a turquoise tail.

I picture the hills where we used to walk,
a brushstroke of clear thought,

our serpentine nature, legs wound together,
making love one early June in Coniston Water.

Life was once bright as a sac of eggs.
You had yet to abandon your art,

turn your frustration into barbed wire
spooled across the gateway to your heart.

I rip up your letters as the ship
swings towards Ellis Island,

stare at the Statue of Liberty
rising out of the mist.

Below Sea Level 1

Sutton on Sea's a thin strip of masking tape,
or a footnote to the sunset
blazing like an early warning - amber, red.
She's an off-season paradise
of fibre-optic water features,
plastic gods and goddesses.
Her avenues and bungalows are criss-crossed
by dykes, ditches, and the Deep Cuts.
Beach huts are bolted for the winter,
faces padlocked against the gales.
A young man with his hood pulled tight
smashes a vodka bottle in the bus stop.
A pensioner takes a J-cloth and wipes
his brassicas clean of sea salt.

Below Sea Level 2

The North Sea lies belly up tonight:
claws sheathed; canines and incisors
tucked in slack, blue-black gums.
She's lapping at shingle, coughing up
the odd bit of plastic, bone or razor clam.
She paws the tanker in the bay — toying with it, this way,
then that. She can take her time, snooze
in the violet evening light, listening for terns.
(She dreams of the storm surge
of '53 when she licked Spurn Head clean.)
Come spring, even her neap tide could breach
the concrete dyke with one swift leap,
spraying the fields of sugar beet,
seething her brine through The Fens.

Mid Summer

Today the temperature drops. Mist hangs over the hills, horses feed in high grass, elderflowers bloom. The fever of summer, its constant sneeze, its red-eye itch, is soothed. Ferns relax. Cats sleep all day on saggy cushions. In the North, politicians argue over warming. We could show them rare butterflies on the moors, swallows arriving a month too early, but not today, not today. Let's find our friends with their lovely round bellies, share a bottle of chardonnay, stuff our afternoon mouths with olives.

Longing is Opened by the Wind

Blocked chimneys become dark throats,
loose tiles moan like sorrow-tongues,

uprooted trees fling their bodies over cars
who crumple at their touch.

Lorries lie upturned in verges,
beside themselves with passion.

The wild brown Calder is in spate,
swallowing her valley whole.

There's a roar of wind and water,
biker-engines at full throttle.

A lighthouse casts out her beam,
scans rough waves off the East Coast.

A ship with dangerous cargo
breaks in two, spews twenty men.

Their hearing is acute for the first time in their lives,
straining for rotating blades to slice the sky with hope,

The news never reports the exact nature of loss.
Metal boxes drift, five fathoms deep,

lodge on the seabed, leaching something
we cannot name into black water.

Airwaves

Angel

*The wings are not flat, but are angled 3.5 degrees forward, which
Gormley says was to create 'a sense of embrace.'*

Once I lay in pieces on a concrete floor,
a colossus modelled from my maker's body.
My core was sunk into the bedrock
like a scientist boring ice.

The wind on my rivets is from Gateshead
and the chemical works at Seal Sands.
I'm the wild cry of seagulls,
the taste of coal, diesel fumes, salt.

One night soon I'll test these fifty-metre wings;
I'll soar with shearwater,
skim the melting polar caps
and kiss the Statue of Liberty.

By sunrise I'll be home.
That's a promise to the *scallys*
who keep me graffiti-free,
the A1 rumbling in my metal bones.

Blackbirds

All that winter she scattered corn at our feet
and we grew fat and lazy as dormice in the hedge.
One morning she clucked us close, then
threw a net, fine as a spider's web.

We fixed her with our yellow eyes
I swear I saw her flinch but, quick as a blade,
she pegged our wings, stuffed us in a sack
that smelt of cats, carried us over her shoulder.

The great iron spit was turning:
all manner of beasts chopped,
mangled, the air laced
with fat and the sickly smell of mead.

Her pretty face was red as a side of pork,
arms dusted with flour. A great slap of pastry
rested on the dresser. She thrust us in together,
twenty four — packed in like slaves in a ship.

I clawed my way to the edge of the crust,
shuddered as the oven slammed shut,
the temperature beginning to climb.
We sang to keep our spirits high.

Just as I began to doze, I felt a breath of air
through a slit in the lid, then the jostling
as we were held up through endless corridors
to the great hall itself.

All that king cares for is gold, taxing his subjects
till they squeal like rats cornered in a midden,
and his wife stuffs her face: honey drizzling
down her well-oiled bosom.

Candlelight and music made us blink,
we raised our beaks and, drunk with air,
we felt the pull of freedom in our wings,
darted for a casement window in the roof.

There she was in the courtyard,
with an armful of sheets
and a mouthful of pegs that had
pinioned my brothers and sisters.

I flew at her: pecked hard at her nose.
She shrieked like a raven
crying for her mate,
bleeding all the way to the castle keep.

Six Swan Brothers

Each baby vanished in the night from the cruck of my arm —
their hair was soft as swallow-breasts.
I sew my nettles together with a fine silver thread.
Each night my fingers bubble with stings. My breath's tight,
like a hare in a sack. I listen to my brothers' throaty calls
over the lake, smell the rush of feathered air.
They come and stand before me in human form
as the sun sets, with their strong thighs, apple-cheeks.
They slap each other on the back; share a jug or two of ale
and smile, (for my sake really). Their shoulders split,
feathers sprout and necks elongate. A darning needle's
pursed between my lips. Each brother has a tongue hard as a skink's.
Let my fingers be nimble. Let my shirts hold together like flax.
I have one green sleeve left to finish.

Rossetti to Lizzie Siddal

I made them dig through earth,
and though the ground was hardened
by the frost, I would have used a pick axe
if my body had been stronger.
Grief had left my bones
brittle as bracken left to over-winter.
The men prised back the lid,
and as I paced the turf,
wood began to crack and splinter.
I thought I find you fast asleep,
your cheeks un-rouged,
hands folded like a pair of ring-necked doves.

Your limbs were blackened:
the air stank of vegetable matter.
Teeth were loose inside your gums,
your eyes were sunken pits.
And yet, my love, your hair
had grown to fill the space
around you like a pool of light.
It rippled in the sun,
and as I bent to hold the weight of it,
I shuddered but I couldn't cry.
My heart became a clod
of sediment inside my chest,
or clay to line a pond,
to hold the water's weight forever.

Crusoe

I've long since lost the ability to speak,
have precious little ink, but my dreams
are coloured by bluebell woods,
white spiked garlic, the astringent green
of new beech, undergrowth bursting
with Fly Agarics, the pungency where puffballs flourish.
Here, tree frogs clamp themselves together in pools,
monkeys howl for mates throughout the night.
I remember my crew with their tropical lusts,
how we spread our semen through girls
with bell-shaped breasts, watched
our lovers drop with the common cold.
I'd give my life to smell the slow,
regular breath of a woman.

Jason

I was there when your child
was born in The North
with his buttermilk skin.

His jaundiced body was bathed
by a sunlamp day and night;
his eyes were swaddled in gauze.

You stroked his wrinkled pelt,
turning and turning the name tag
loose about his wrist.

And you were wild with love for him,
wild with lack of sleep, hospital gown
flapping like swans' wings.

Now he's lean and gangly
with a shock of curls
and a camera strapped around his chest.

His life is a sea-chart
laid out before him, marked
with towering rocks, submerged wrecks.

Your son's forefinger traces
coastlines, continents, in search
of his crew, dreaming of his fleece.

High Pressure

I'm in a hammock in the garden
clutching Alice Hoffman's latest novel,
the lawn burnt to a tinder.
The thought of you is a tear welling up.
High pressure bursts. A downpour washes
leaves clean of dust.

My headache lifts like a red kite.
And you're curled in your London flat
on a black sofa stuffed tight with feathers.
You had seven good eggs to choose from,
Hope had been a rising line of mercury in the heat.
Outside your window, tarmac bubbles,

the Capital's green lungs are
crammed with lovers. You text me.
IVF failed. No joy this time. As kids, we tested
our sense of balance on the see-saw in Congleton park,
grey pleated skirts billowed like shuttlecocks,
one up, one down.

It's always been this way. I got pregnant
as simply as a jump from a swing.
You're thirty-nine, inject your stomach
till it blooms purple, then yellow.
Through the skylight, you watch a plane tree
flaming before winter.

Incubating Twins

She strokes their stomachs with her forefinger.
Tomorrow or the next day,
their small sarcophagi will be opened forever.
She will hold their wee bodies to the sun,
breathe their scent, like freshly-cut hay.

Breast-milk stains her blue silk gown.
Robert screams when she has to go home.
She carries his cry like a wren in her pocket.
Feels the sharp beak of it.
Throughout the night, she sings to them
across the streets of Lewisham.

Chinese Fire Bellied Newt

You are as delicate as an unborn thing —
a glutinous chick in its sac, or the twelve week
scan of my boy with his spine curled like a question mark.

You raise your head towards me, slowly
nosing up glass, feet like plastic suckers.
You display a silk waistcoat: imperial orange and black.

I am drawn back to the first fish that gulped air,
sulphurous mud clinging,
eyes bulging at an ocean of green.

Today your S-shaped tail is wedged
between a pebble and the aquarium base. You leap
across open water, miniature arms outstretched,

ready to embrace, toxic to the touch.
I'm aware of my coccyx, lack of fur,
my love of diving into a salty pool.

Premature

I'm kept in a box. I blink.
Smell hot plastic. Stretch out my hand
to watch a pattern of light redden.
I'm a glow-in-the-dark; half-fish
with slithery lungs in a ribcage supple as a slipper.
My skull's pointed, yet to harden.
My hold on life is lax.

Mother's face rises like a full moon
and her eyes cloud over with green.
I've lost her metronome heartbeat.
I've no idea of the comfort of her milk-tipped
nipple, nor the crook of her arm,
nor the rhythm of a walk in the park
with sycamore leaves to soften the sun's stare.

Lost

I have forgotten hours heaving with sickness,
sinuses stuffed with mucus,

the taste of rusty metal,
my yellow, swollen ankles,

the shock of the blue-cross test,
the thumbscrews of distress.

And I have forgotten all ambivalence
because I lost you.

Postcard to My Mother

I sat down and wept in a white-tiled room
whilst a soft flop
                    slipped into a cardboard bowl
and was whisked away by a nurse.
Her apron was starched with distaste.

She scraped my belly clean
like a dish of stew left to sour in the fridge,
mould lacing the edge and meat turned bad.

How I long
for the cadence of your voice:
Hush now child, it's nae worth all this blither.

Unborn Daughter

I see her at the edge of things —
wrapped in spider-silk before the abbey stirs,
or curled in the belly of a Wharfedale sheep
safe in the hollow of a hawthorn hedge.

I hear her crying from another mother's pram
or nodding her damp head.
Maybe she's strapped to her father's chest
in a pouch as he strides across the stepping stones.

I smell her in the warmth of a pillow
pressed to my swollen breasts —
At night, she swims
to kiss me through the The Strid's turbulence.

Open Season

28th December 2007

Stubbled men in flak-jackets
caught my eye, but didn't speak,
snares tucked under their arms.

The mole-catcher, with his heart-shaped
spade and battered Rover
grinned as he swung my gate wide.

The Sweep told me the mid-feathers were fucked,
shoved a body he'd plucked from the chimney
into my arms, wings stiff with frost.

Outside, the air was cordite-thick.
Shots boomeranged across the moors.
Beaters were out in force, spattered in peat.

I was failing to light a fire;
flicked the switch on the radio.
The world tilted East.

Benazir's voice was tremulous.
She waved from her Land Cruiser:
I've been waiting for clear skies.
Pakistan is in my blood.

A pheasant stuttered out of the beech wood.
A poor flyer, she grazed a car bonnet
before crash-landing in the thicket.

Runswick Bay

A stranger has pitched a tent right on the edge,
strung out his washing
like Tibetan prayer flags
as turf cleaves away from the bedrock.

A bunker has crashed head-first onto sand.
Bats dive-bomb us, flitting in
and out of concrete slits, searching
for that damp square of safety, a way inside.

U boats once patrolled this horizon,
ready to torpedo Scarborough.
Our grandmother surveyed the water,
arms folded, her fiancée *Lost in Action*.

My lungs are ripe plums splitting
as we climb out of the bay.
Suddenly a tawny owl swoops over tarmac,
picks off a pipistrelle, wings soft as vowels.

Across a continent, men hardly speak,
lie with bellies pressed to the floor like frogs,
scanning Helmand's poppy fields
with their night-vision screens.

Ghandi visits Café Nero, Boar Lane, Leeds.

The waitress is selling pastries stuffed with almond paste.
I don't notice him at first, but then catch sight of his feet,
those calloused heels. He shivers in a strip of linen,
glasses steaming in the heat. Customers are staring.
A couple move away from the smell of sour skin.
He orders water, then turns to me and holds out his hand.
I place a warm pound in his palm;
he smiles and tilts his head. The girl tuts.
We're trying to discourage them,
the money only gets spent on drink.
He takes a sip of water and leans his staff
against the Panini cabinet, sits cross-legged
in the queue and doesn't speak.
I wish a ripple of commuters in their pin-stripes
would sit beside him, fanning out over the city —
a wave of disobedience.

Unwanted Guest

Like the Goddess Hydra, some of our organs
can replicate. Our skin takes two weeks,
our livers are old as toddlers.

Others struggle. With us for the long haul.
The lens of an eye thickens, type blurs
as if viewed through a basin of water.

You'd got round to reading Tolstoy,
French doors opened to retirement's orchard,
when the doctor placed

the C word in your lap.
A calling card from a relative
you'd loathed all your life.

Coach Journey, Innsbruck

We hair-pin through the Alps
and sickness is a dog lurching in my stomach.

I smell sour, but my father stays by my side
on the grass verge whilst my sisters

catch a cable-car up to the glacier,
whooping with delight.

Maybe I sit on his knee for a while
or maybe we wander through a village

of gingerbread houses
to reach a meadow where the air is sweet.

Gentians are jewelling the ground.
This blue is Happiness.

My sisters dangle their fat legs
high above the mountain; peer into its heart.

I fold my father into my cable-knit cardigan.

Oberammergau

I'm in my Sunday Best — dwarfed
by a wooden cross on the outdoor stage.
The Passion Play opens this Easter,
and a man has just been chosen to play Jesus.

Gethsemane is painted on a backcloth
brilliant with palms, lemon trees and vines.
A polystyrene rock is poised at the entrance to the cave.
Kettle-drum mountains amplify sound.

I drop a coin as we tour the amphitheatre.
My song echoes round the hillside.
I imagine Mary Magdalene crying *He is risen,*
He is risen, with her arms flung open.

The audience murmurs as she oils his feet,
bent over with the smell of love,
hair plastered to her cheeks. For the rest of us,
resurrection is a bluebird, or a unicorn.

When I'm eleven my father is gone
into the garden and I'm deemed
too young to see his body laid out,
to stroke his paper-thin skin.

I'm still praying for that rush of air
as a door creaks open, his white shirt
smelling of a long, hot day
and his car engine cooling on the drive.

Lake Louise

Glaciers are dirt-stained cheeks
retreating back into high lands

like the childhood memory of a father,
his imprint, the hollow *cirque* of him

pressed onto his daughter's mind.

The spruce-covered valley is the
U-shaped song
they used to hum together

scooped out between mountains
ice holding the shape
of an ancient flow of kinship

There's no name for this blue milk
of lake-the colour of a sob

held so long in the chest,
a terminal moraine.

Hibernation

A freight train hoots at a level crossing.
Somewhere up Mount Rundle,
a grizzly and her cub lift their snouts
to snow in the air. Stomachs fat with berries,
they'll soon head into the last scrap
of forest, curl round each other like cochlea.

How I long for a den. A place to over-winter,
a bracken-scented nest,
deep sleep that slows the pulse.
I would bury my phone and my computer,
find an old garage for the Skoda,
let my body live off subcutaneous layers.

Come spring, I'd emerge thin and ready
for a fuck with my lover,
for a draft of strong coffee as the earth heats up.

Alleyway

We're standing on a narrow road in the core of the city, an intersection with Northumberland St. You kiss me and I'm struck by the neatness of the way we fit together, hip bone to hip bone, how familiar you taste even though I barely know the smell of your skin, struck by the way my body can relax against you, lose that stiffness, how I always hold my breath, forget to use the capacity for love in my lungs. Colonnaded banks and offices tower above our heads and we're still stuck together, snogging in the middle of King Street beyond the safety of the pavement's edge.

We could be mown down by careless road-users that litter our past — bikers, speeders, van drivers who we've entrusted with our hearts, marked us with tyre-treads of disappointment; my overhead-twin-cam obsessed ex, your MG Midget-woman with the sporty smile.

You smell of city-warmth, yeasty dark ale, and I'm dripping like oil leaking from a sump, nipples hard as nickel against the wool of your coat and we're still kissing on tarmac, with the Beatles lyric, 'Why don't we do it in the road' racing through our heads.

Forcing Shed

*Rhubarb was revered for its mysterious cathartic powers. Today, a small
community of farms in Yorkshire's 'Rhubarb Triangle' keeps some of these
secrets alive.*

Rain soaked their trainers the day they met —
her nipples stood out like stalks through her jumper.

They broke into his old man's forcing shed,
fumbled each other in a forest of grooved sugar.

They could hear shoots unfurl in the gloom, straining for light.
She were plastered with leaves, aching for summer.

He found a moon-shaped pebble that smelt of vinegar,
cradled it in the lining of his school blazer

as she locked herself into a wardrobe at night.
The stone was shot through with quartz

like that razor blade she used to stripe her skin.
He thought all his love

would blanket her from this,
but — like a splinter — her secret pressed further in.

Adultery

Unshaven, the husband stumbles onto the lawn
when the dew is heavy, the privet black and glossy leaved.
Grass-cuttings steam from the compost heap
in the early morning light.

There's a white-faced rush of air, a vole's skitter,
                              the skull's crunch.

This man bides his time like a blunt-nosed pike
lurking below the overhang of the riverbank,
observes the cork-screw currents from beneath —
his mayfly-wife's delicate, dangerous dance.

Love in Snowdonia

Tree

We met in July when the damson tree
bore fruit for the first time in ten years,
each branch heavy with velvety clusters.

We pricked skins, crushed brown candy sugar,
added gin to kilner jars,
lined our oak cupboard with liquid *trysor*

Rain

drumming on slate
signalled the end of the heat wave.
Our whisky smelt of larch and heather,

cheeks flushed, wood spitting in the grate,
your skin tasted of purple
smoke, freshly dug earth.

Candle

I walk from room to room
pick up stubby pencils, shells, iron nails
holding in the breath

that we let out in long gasps.

At night I keep a candle
burning on the ledge,

light spilling across the fields.

A&S Forever

The dinosaurs went extinct on Christmas Eve, and humans started roaming the earth at 8:30 p.m. on New Year's Eve.

Grief is carboniferous. All those ferns compacted
by the earth's geological flower press.

The Derbyshire delta unfolds
meadows of cartilage and bone.

To the west, I can see Jodrell Bank.
An upturned bowl listening for a dead star's pulse.

Loss is millstone grit. Wildboar Clough
knuckled clean by wind and rain.

Its language is measured in eons; charting the rise
and fall of ice sheets, dinosaurs, now ourselves.

And our life together is a green-eyed blink
or two snails in the shadow of a boot.

Hand me a chisel and hammer,
let me carve *A&S forever*

into stone whilst I watch the slow
passage of the river.

Touched

I search the house for traces of you,
a finger mark on architrave,
measurements in soft pencil-scrawl,
the plaster curve in my stairwell
smooth as a woman's inner thigh.

Each mitred joint,
each fine grade sanded corner,
each door frame
carries your imprint.
There's the faintest smell of us

lingering in the sawdust,
in the attic shadows.
You may catch me
when the house is still,
wearing nothing but lipstick
and smiling, pressing
my body to the floor.

Slug Language

Kitchen. 3 a.m.

Pure tongue,
their bodies write out
the glow of a pearly button
burst from a pale silk shift,
the sheen of a vulva.

They have criss-crossed my lino
all night, wound together like a nest of snakes
to smear the soles of my feet
with their silver calligraphy.

I print the whole house with desire.

After kissing him out into the night

She can feel the kettle of his fingers on her buttocks, his tongue's flex as it stroked the edge of her top teeth, hooked her in, her hips imprinted with the zip of his combat pants.

The kitchen fills with the bitterness of Drum tobacco or a burnt out fuse somewhere in the cellar. His silhouette is still there, edged with static in the doorway: a wet-leaved space smelling of Rioja left to stand in a glass.

She can taste his forearm's salt, like the wet fur of cats curled together on a chair. He's there on the rim of still-warm coffee cup or chocolate smeared in the rug where he sat cross-legged and listened to *La Mer*.

Lilies wind up the stairs: their throats glisten, showering the carpet with saffron. The whole fucking house glows like a lava lamp.

Kist

A coffin is cut from the hill,
close to its core, licked clean by wind.

The skeleton lies in a foetal curl,
tibia tucked towards her ribs,

joints worn smooth as stone,
tarsals and meta-tarsals delicate as lace.

There's her pelvis. Small as my own,
a bone-cradle where a child
might have nestled like a bird.

Did her body cleave to her lover's?

Were her breasts once kissed as you kiss mine,
peat smoke scorching our throats?

We gasp at her plait. The way it falls
where her cheek once pressed itself into the earth.

Hair makes her real to us, preserved
in this anaerobic space we disturb with our breath.

Flight

She is a gyroscope, thrumming
on the centre of a taut string
held between your fingers.

She is a hot air balloon
tethered in a parched field.
One blast of fire,
brightly coloured silk will leave you grounded.

National Poetry Day, Edge Hill School

Turning and turning in the widening gyre
                                    'The Second Coming' W.B.Yeats.

It's twenty to three. Outside, crows are circling.
Year Nine no longer look at me,
or take trouble over their words. They're skittery,
like a flock of woolly-backs, sensing that Time is a sheepdog
sliding under the five bar gate. The room stinks
and the Head of English has deserted us.
Darren pops gum on his bruised lip, Shane sends his pen
cart-wheeling towards my left wrist. *I'm done now, Miss.*
I can't stand f'ing poetry. I could hand out rough justice,
but I reach for Yeats and manage to recite four lines
without checking the wretched textbook, its spine
spitting all the pages out. *What's anarchy, is that like Punk?*
Here's a lull just before the bell rings,
a silence the colour of a lion's pelt.

When the time comes

drive me into Wynatt's pass
remind me of the names of caverns;
Treakcliffe, Speedwell, The Devil's Throat,
the hollow nature of the earth.

Take me over the Shivering Mountain
to the valley where they named a village Hope,
close-cropped fields blooming with
Spotted Orchid, Eye Bright, Lady's Slipper.

On to home turf. Surround me
with a feathered quilt of friends,
then shoo them out. Feed me slivers of
ripe mango, find a way to swiftly chill Chablis.

Weave me a coffin made from willow,
root out my bright pink stilettos,
give each guest a plant from my garden,
cut lavender to the quick, crush it over my fingers.

Promise to adopt the cats,
let my son choose his favourite aunt for a mother,
a cousin for a brother, unlock
all the windows of the house to let the sky soak in.

You can say what you like to The Dead

                    but talking to the living
is a shout down a mobile as you enter a tunnel.
You need courage and a clear signal.
Resist the urge to redefine
a half-heard message that crackles with love
then fizzles as the world goes black.

I've always been the kind of woman
who wants to end other peoples' phrases,
to second guess. I know it's a bad habit.
Don't text me — it's too brief,
like being offered
one red Smartie from a tube.

We all need tracks to each other,
the criss-cross of an island-hopping ferry
or we end up strange: like the duck-billed platypus —
all fur and flippers — or Galapagos dragons
left to spit salt water in their own
dead end in the Mid-Pacific.

So ring me often. Let me wallow in the cadence
of your voice. Let me download my day's
inconsequence: the plumber who never showed up,
the lack of fat cheques on the doormat,
the orchid in bloom by my bed and the sight of a hare
bursting from its scrape like a cry for help.

Notes

Love in Snowdonia: *trysor* is Welsh for 'treasure'.